New Chinese for Children
新儿童汉语 ①

编著：刘 珣 张亚军 丁永寿

插图：赵倩倩 吴延明 等 英译：张 耘

Compiled by: Liu Xun
　　　　　　 Zhang Yajun
　　　　　　 Ding Yongshou

Illustrated by: Zhao Qianqian
　　　　　　　 Wu Yanming et al.

Translated by: Zhang Yun

华语教学出版社
SINOLINGUA

First Edition 2011

ISBN 978-7-5138-0082-2
Copyright 2011 by Sinolingua
Published by Sinolingua
24 Baiwanzhuang Road, Beijing 100037, China
Tel:(86)10-68320585, 68997826
Fax:(86)10-68997826, 68320585
http://www.sinolingua.com.cn
E-mail: hyjx@sinolingua.com.cn
Printed by Sanhe Huixin Printing Co.,Ltd.

Printed in the People's Republic of China

致老师和家长们

《新儿童汉语》是为 3～12 岁的外国儿童学习汉语准备的初级读本。

本套教材分为 3 册，每册 20 课。第一册以语音为主，反复进行四声的基本功训练。第二、三册主要介绍汉语的一些基本句式，浅显易懂。每册后附有词汇表和辅导材料。词汇表收录的词语，遵循常用程度和重要性编排。辅导材料为中英文对照，对各课的语法点作了说明，是老师和家长的好帮手。

本套教材突出实用的原则，从儿童日常生活中最熟悉的事物入手，教给他们生活中使用最多的一些词汇，让他们学会说一些简单的生活用语。教材体现了较强的趣味性，选取儿童感兴趣的话题，反映儿童自己的生活。教材的主人公是中国和外国的孩子，内容上体现了儿童生活的特点，如课文中有游戏，小孩"过家家"，小兔、小狗、孙悟空，以及做梦到月亮上去旅行的情节等。

本套教材全部采用对话形式，并适当穿插一些谜语、儿歌、游戏、图画，形式活泼，语言生动，图文并茂。

学完这三册书后，小读者们能掌握 300 多个汉语词汇，以及一些最基本的语言材料，为将来系统、正规地学习汉语打下基础。

为了使您的孩子能准确地掌握发音，我们为本套教材配备了标准普通话录音光盘。

编者

2011 年 4 月

To Teachers and Parents

New Chinese for Children is a series of elementary textbooks specifically designed to teach Chinese to children overseas who are three to twelve years old.

There are three books in all, each consisting of twenty lessons. Book 1 is aimed at teaching children correct Chinese pronunciation and the four tones through a wide range of pronunciation exercises; books 2 and 3deal mainly with basic sentence patterns, all of which are simple and can be easily understood by children. Each book has an appendix that includes Teacher's Notes and a Vocabulary List. The Vocabulary List covers the key words used in daily communication by children. The bilingual Teacher's Notes explain the grammar points of each lesson and will be a useful guide for teachers and parents.

This series takes a practical approach to teaching, presenting the children with the familiar words and phrases that are most used in their everyday lives. The topics chosen will be interesting to children because they focus on a child's daily life; the leading characters in the books are all children, both Chinese and foreign, who talk about bunnies and doggies, games such as playing house, tell each other stories like the Monkey King and talk about the journeys they have taken to the moon in their dreams.

The texts are in the form of dialogues, and are enlivened by riddles, nursery rhymes, games and drawings. Lively language, together with a large number of illustrations, make this book appealing to children.

After completing this series, children will have a basic knowledge of the Chinese language that will include pronunciation, a vocabulary of over 300 words, and basic sentence patterns, which will lay a solid foundation for future Chinese language study.

To better help children in learning to pronounce Chinese correctly, we have included accompanying CDs to the texts.

The Compilers
April, 2011

Contents

bàba

daddy

māma

mummy

gēge

elder brother

dìdi

younger brother

b d g   α e i

Who are they?

āyí	**bóbo**
auntie	uncle

Āyí hǎo!	Hello, auntie!
Bóbo hǎo!	Hello, uncle!
Nín hǎo!	Hello ! / How are you?

o ao in

_____ hǎo!

_____ hǎo!

ā	á	ǎ	à
bō	bó	bǒ	bò
gē	gé	gě	gè

Characters to learn

好   good, well, fine

hǎo

3

mèimei
younger sister

wǒ
I

māo
cat

gǒu
dog

ei ou

Bàba hǎo!　Māma ＿＿＿＿＿＿＿＿＿!

ā	á	ǎ	à
(mēi)	méi	měi	mèi
gōu	(góu)	gǒu	gòu

Characters to learn

我　I, me

wǒ

6

4

píngguǒ
apple

pútao
grape

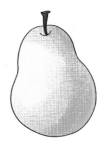

lí
pear

Wǒ yào pútao.	I want some grapes.
Dìdi yào píngguǒ.	My younger brother wants an apple.
Mèimei yào lí.	My younger sister wants a pear.

What do you want?

Wǒ yào _____.

What does your sister want?

_____.

ā	á	ǎ	à
pū	pú	pǔ	pù
tāo	táo	tǎo	tào

Characters to learn

苹 果 apple

píng guǒ

5

dàngāo	bǐnggān	táng	kāfēi
cake	biscuit	sweets	coffee

Gēge yào kāfēi.
    My elder brother wants some coffee.

Dìdi yào táng.
    My younger brother wants sweets.

Mèimei yào bǐnggān.
    My younger sister wants biscuits.

Wǒ yào dàngāo, wǒ bú yào kāfēi.
    I want some cakes, I don't want coffee.

p t k   an ang

What does he want?

Dìdi yào _____ ,

bú yào _____ .

_____ ,

_____ .

ā   á   ǎ   à

kā   (ká)   kǎ   kà

tāng táng tǎng tàng

gān (gán) gǎn gàn

Characters to learn

不   not, no   要   to want

bù   yào

Nǐmen hǎo

Bà ba hǎo, mā ma hǎo, bà ba mā ma nǐ men hǎo.

Bó bo hǎo, ā yí hǎo, bó bo ā yí nǐ men hǎo.

Can you read them?

a	gā-kā	gǒu-guǒ
o	bó-pó	nín-níng
e	gē-kē	tán-táng
i	dì-tì	
u	bú-pú	pào-pèi

What will they say?

6

chá
tea

niúnǎi
milk

Zhè shì chá.	This is tea.
Zhè shì niúnǎi.	This is milk.
Gēge yào niúnǎi ma?	Does your elder brother want some milk?
Gēge bú yào niúnǎi.	No, he doesn't.
Tā yào chá.	He wants some tea.

zh ch sh iu ai

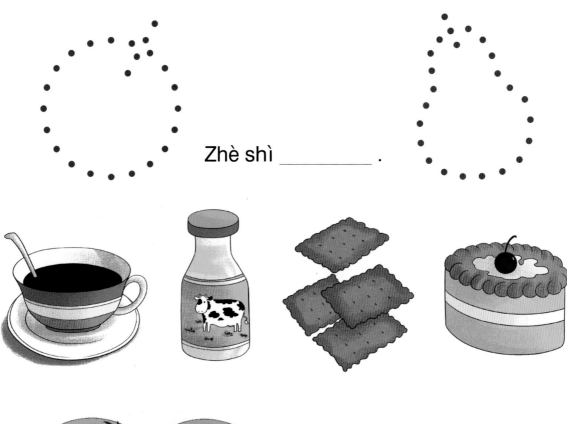

Zhè shì _____ .

zhē	zhé	zhě	zhè
chā	chá	chǎ	chà
shī	shí	shǐ	shì

Characters to learn

这 this   是 to be   他 he, him

zhè   shì   tā

7

miànbāo
bread

miàntiáo
noodles

niúròu
beef

zhōu
porridge

Zhè shì niúròu.

This is beef.

Wǒ yào miànbāo, bú yào niúròu.

I want some bread, I don't want beef.

Nǐ yào zhōu ma?

Do you want some porridge?

Wǒ bú yào zhōu, Wǒ yào miàntiáo.

No, I don't. I want some noodles.

zh ch sh r ian iao

What are they?

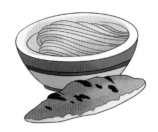

Zhè shì _____ .

Ask questions

_____ ?

Wǒ yào pútao.

_____ ?

Wǒ bú yào niúnǎi.

zhī	zhí	zhǐ	zhì
chī	chí	chǐ	chì
(rōu)	róu	rǒu	ròu

Characters to learn

你 you
nǐ

面包 bread
miàn bāo

8

Zhè shì lǎoshī.   This is the teacher.
Lǎoshī hǎo!   Good morning, sir!
Nà shì gōngrén shūshu.   That is a worker.
Shūshu hǎo!   Hello, uncle!
Nǐ hǎo!   Hello!

Lǎoshī teacher

gōngrén worker

Yéye hǎo!
    Good afternoon, grandpa!
Nǎinai hǎo!
    Good afternoon, grandma!

yéye grandpa
nǎinai grandma

zh ch sh r ong en

What will you say?

Shūshu _____ !

Āyí _____ !

Who are they?

_____

_____

shū	shú	shǔ	shù
(rēn)	rén	rěn	rèn
gōng	(góng)	gǒng	gòng

Characters to learn

那   that
nà

叔叔   uncle
shū shu

9

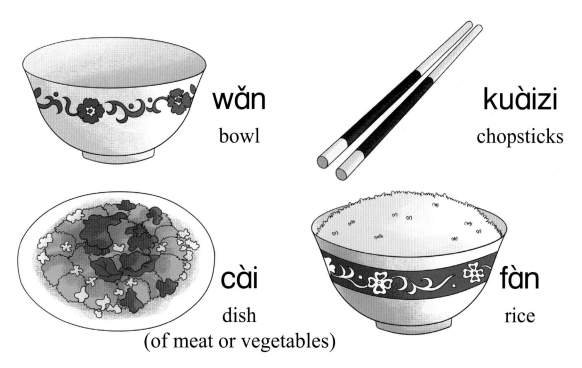

wǎn
bowl

kuàizi
chopsticks

cài
dish
(of meat or vegetables)

fàn
rice

Zhè shì shénme?	What is this?
Zhè shì wǎn.	This is a bowl.
Nà shì shénme?	What is that?
Nà shì kuàizi.	That is a pair of chopsticks.
Zhè shì shénme?	What is this?
Zhè shì cài.	It's a dish of meat.
Nà shì shénme?	What is that?
Nà shì fàn.	That is rice.

z c   uai

Zhè shì shénme? _____ . Zhè shì shénme? _____ .

Nà shì shénme? _____ . Nà shì shénme? _____ .

Ask questions

_____ ? Zhè shì píngguǒ. _____ ? Zhè shì kuàizi.

_____ ? Nà shì lí. _____ ? Nà shì fàn.

zī	(zí)	zǐ	zì
cī	cí	cǐ	cì
cāi	cái	cǎi	cài

Characters to learn

什 么 what 饭 rice

shén me fàn

10

huā   yèzi   cǎo   shù   sēnlín

flower   leaf   grass   tree   forest

Zhè shì shénme?	What is this?
Zhè shì huā.	This is a flower.
Nà shì shénme?	What is that?
Nà shì yèzi.	That is a leaf.
Nà bú shì huā, nà shì cǎo.	That is not a flower. That is grass.
Zhè shì shù.	This is a tree.
Nà shì sēnlín.	That is a forest.

sī   (sí)   sǐ   sì
sēn   (sén)   (sěn) (sèn)
cāo   cáo   cǎo   (cào)

Characters to learn

花 flower   树 tree   草 grass
huā   shù   cǎo

Zhè shì lǎbahuā

Zhè shì shén me shù? Zhè shì

píng guǒ shù. Zhè shì shén me huā?

Zhè shì lǎ ba huā, zhè shì lǎ ba huā.

note: lǎbahuā   morning-glory

zhī-zī-tī   mái-méi

chí-cí-pí   kài-kuài

shǐ-sǐ-bǐ   sān-sēn

rì-sì-dì   lǒu-liǔ

When your friend comes to your home....

Zhè shì wǒ bàba .

_____ .

_____ .

_____ .

Questions and answers

11

zhuōzi
desk

yǐzi
chair

chuáng
bed

shūbāo
satchel

sǎn
umbrella

Wǒ yǒu zhuōzi, yǒu yǐzi, yǒu chuáng.

I have a desk, a chair and a bed.

Zhè shì shénme? Zhè shì shūbāo.

What's this? This is a satchel.

Nà shì shénme? Nà shì sǎn.

What's that? That is an umbrella.

What does he/she have?

Mèimei yǒu _____ .

Gēge yǒu _____ .

Characters to learn

有 to have
yǒu

书 包 satchel
shū bāo

12

fēijī	qìchè	lúnchuán	zìxíngchē
plane	car	ship	bike

Nǐ yǒu fēijī ma?   Do you have a plane?

    Wǒ yǒu fēijī.   Yes, I have.

    Dìdi yǒu qìchē.   My younger brother has a car.

    Mèimei yǒu lúnchuán.   My younger sister has a ship.

    Jiějie yǒu zìxíngchē.   My elder sister has a bike.

Bāba zàijiàn!   Bye-bye, dad!

Māma zàijiàn!   Bye-bye, mum!

j q x   un uan ie

Ask questions

_____?

Bàba yǒu qìchē.

_____?

Wǒ yǒu zìxíngchē.

What will you say?

Shūshu, āyí _____ !

Lǎoshī _____ .

jī	jí	jǐ	jì
qī	qí	qǐ	qì
xī	xí	xǐ	xì
jiē	jié	jiě	jiè

Characters to learn

吗 an interrogative particle

ma

再 见 bye-bye

zài jiàn

13

jīqìrén	wáwa	píqiú	xióngmāo
robot	doll	ball	panda

Wǒ yǒu jīqìrén, wǒ méiyǒu qìchē.

I have a robot. I don't have a car.

Dìdi yǒu qìchē, dìdi méiyǒu píqiú.

My younger brother has a car. He doesn't have a ball.

Mèimei yǒu wáwa, tā méiyǒu píqiú.

My younger sister has a doll. She doesn't have a ball.

Jiějie méiyǒu wáwa, tā yǒu xióngmāo.

My elder sister doesn't have a doll. She has a panda.

j q x   iong

What do you have?

Wǒ yǒu _____ .

Wǒ méiyǒu _____ .

Dìdi yǒu _____ .

Tā méiyǒu _____ .

Mèimei yǒu _____ .

Tā méiyǒu _____ .

Gēge yǒu _____ .

Tā méiyǒu _____ .

Characters to learn

她 she, her

tā

皮 球 ball

pí qiú

14

zhōngguó
China

guóqí
national flag

Běijīng
Beijing

Tiān'ānmén
Tian'anmen

Chángchéng
the Great Wall

Māma, zhè shì guóqí ma?

   Zhè shì guóqí.

   Zhè shì Zhōngguó guóqí.

Nà shì shénme?

   Nà shì Tiān'ānmén.

Zhè shì Chángchéng ma?

   Zhè shì Chángchéng.

Is this a national flag, mum?

   Yes, it is.

   It's the national flag of China.

What's that?

   That's Tian'anmen.

Is this the Great Wall?

   This is the Great Wall.

j q x   eng

Answer the questions

Zhè shì kuàizi ma?

_____ .

Zhè shì yǐzi ma?

_____ .

Ask questions

_____ ?

Zhè shì chuáng.

_____ ?

Zhè shì sǎn.

Characters to learn

中 国 China
Zhōng guó

妈 妈 mum, mummy
mā ma

32

yǔ

rain

Xià yǔ le.

It's raining.

xuě

snow

Xià xuě le.

It's snowing.

wù

fog

Xià wù le.

It's foggy.

fēng

wind

Guā fēng le.

It's windy.

ü üe ia

What is the weather like?

 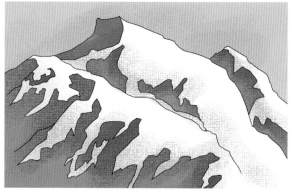

yū   yú   yǔ   yù
xuē   xué   xuě   xuè
xiā   xiá   (xiǎ) xià

Characters to learn

下 to fall
xià

雪 snow
xuě

了 a particle
le

Xiǎo māo zěnyàng jiào

Wǒ　　ài　　wǒ de　xiǎo māo.　Xiǎo māo　zěn yàng　jiào?

Wǒ　　ài　　wǒ de　xiǎo gǒu.　Xiǎo gǒu　zěn yàng　jiào?

Wǒ　　ài　　wǒ de　wáwa.　　 Wá wa　　zěn yàng　xiào?

Miao　miao　miao,　miao miao miao,　miao miao miao miao miao!

Wang wang wang,　wang wang wang,　wang wang wang wang wang!

　Ha　ha　ha,　ha ha ha,　　ha　ha　ha　ha　ha!

I love my kitten.　　How does my kitten mew?

I love my puppy.　　How does my puppy bark?

I love my doll.　　 How does my doll laugh?

Can you read them?

jī-qī-xī   nǔ-nǚ

zì-cì-sì   chuán-chuáng

zhí-chí-shí   jiē-juē

                 xíng-xióng

When you want something...

Māma, yǒu píngguǒ ma?   _____?

Wǒ yào píngguǒ.   _____.

16

tàiyáng

the sun

yuèliang

the moon

yún

cloud

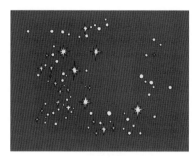

xīngxing

star

hóng

rainbow

Nà shì tàiyáng ma?
    Nà bú shì tàiyáng,
    nà shì yuèliang.
Nà shì yún ma?
    Nà bú shì yún,
    nà shì hóng.
Nà shì xīngxing ma?
    Nà bú shì xīngxing,
    nà shì dēng.

Is that the sun?
    No, it isn't.
    It's the moon.
Is that a cloud?
    No, that's not a cloud.
    That's a rainbow.
Is that a star?
    That's not a star.
    That's a lamp.

ün iang

Answer the questions

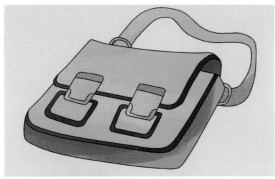

Zhè shì shūbāo ma?

_____.

Zhè shì lǎoshī ma?

_____.

Ask questions

_____?

Zhè bú shì guóqí.

_____?

Zhè bú shì fēijī.

_____?

Zhè bú shì lúnchuán.

Characters to learn

太 阳   the sun

tài yáng

灯   light, lamp

dēng

17

 **ěrduo**
ear

 bízi
nose

 **yǎnjing**
eye

 **zuǐ**
mouth

 **shǒu**
hand

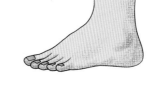 **jiǎo**
foot

Zhè shì ěrduo ma?
  Is this an ear?

Zhè bú shì ěrduo, zhè shì yǎnjing.
  No, this isn't an ear. It's an eye.

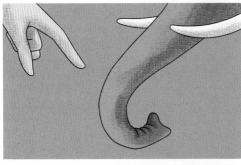

Zhè shì zuǐ ma?
  Is this a mouth?

Zhè bú shì zuǐ, zhè shì bízi.
  No, this isn't a mouth. It is a nose.

Zhè shì shénme?
  What is this?

Zhè shì shǒu.
  This is a hand.

Jīqìrén yǒu jiǎo ma? Jīqìrén yǒu jiǎo.
  Does the robot have feet?
  Yes, the robot has feet.

er ui

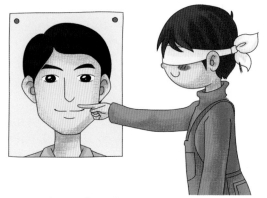

Zhè shì yǎnjing ma?

_____ .

Zhè shì shénme?

_____ .

Zhè shì bízi ma?

_____ .

Zhè shì shénme?

_____ .

Play a game

Characters to learn

手 hand

shǒu

眼 睛 eye

yǎn jing

18

shǒutàor

gloves

shǒujuànr

handkerchief

xié

shoes

shàng yī

jacket

kùzi

trousers

qúnzi

skirt

yīfu

clothes

Zhè shì wǒ de yīfu.
   This is my clothes.

Nà shì dìdi de kùzi.
   Those are my younger brother's trousers.

Zhè shì jiějie de shǒutàor.
   These are my elder sister's gloves.

Nà shì mèimei de xié.
   Those are my younger sister's shoes.

Zhè shì nǐ de shǒujuànr ma?
   Is this your handkerchief ?

Zhè bú shì wǒ de shǒujuànr.
   No, it isn't.

Zhè shì bàba de shǒujuànr.
   It's my dad's.

üan

Zhè shì bàba de yīfu ma?

_____ .

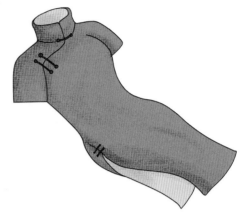

Zhè shì māma de yīfu ma?

_____ .

Zhè shì lǎoshī de shūbāo ma?

_____ .

Zhè shì māo de ěrduo ma?

_____ .

Zhè shì gēge de xié ma?

_____ .

Characters to learn

的 a structural particle
de

衣 服 clothes
yī fu

19

shū
book

huàr
picture

bǐ
pen

Wǒ kàn shū,
   dìdi huà huàr.
Gēge, nǐ yǒu bǐ ma?
   Wǒ yǒu bǐ. Nǐ yào ma?
Yào.
   Gěi nǐ.
Xièxie.

I am reading a book.
   My younger brother is painting a picture.
Brother, do you have a pen?
   Yes, I have. Do you want it?
Yes.
   Here you are.
Thanks.

Gěi nǐ píngguǒ.
Xièxie māma.

Gěi nǐ wáwa.
Xièxie āyí.

Characters to learn

看 to see, to read　kàn

书 book　shū

画儿 picture　huàr

20

qǐchuáng
to get up

chàng gēr
to sing

tiàowǔ
to dance

xué Hànyǔ
to learn Chinese

zuò yóuxì
to play games

shuìjiào
to sleep

Wǒmen chàng gēr.
Wǒmen tiàowǔ.
Wǒmen zuò yóuxì.
Wǒmen xué Hànyǔ.

Characters to learn

我 们 we, us   学 to learn   汉 语 Chinese (language)

wǒ men   xué   Hàn yǔ

Wǒmen xué Hànyǔ

Wǒ   men   chàng gē, wǒ men tiào   wǔ.

Wǒ   men   zuò yóu xì,   wǒ men xué Hàn yǔ.

La la la la   la la la,   la la la la   la la la.

Wǒ   men   zuò yóu xì,   wǒ men xué Hàn   yǔ.

Can you read them?

ia-ua-uo   ie-üe

uai-ui   iao-iu

ian-uan-üan   in-un-ün

iang-uang-ueng   ing-iong

What are these?

皮球   衣服   眼睛

树   书

面包   太阳   手

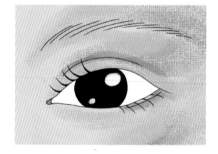 

Can you write these characters?

妈_____   他_____   花_____

好_____   你_____   草_____

她_____   什么_____   苹果_____

词汇表
Vocabulary List

B

不	bù	not, no

C

草	cǎo	grass

D

的	de	a structural particle
灯	dēng	light, lamp

F

饭	fàn	rice

H

汉语	Hànyǔ	Chinese (language)
好	hǎo	good, well, fine
花	huā	flower
画儿	huàr	picture

K

看	kàn	to see, to look to watch, to read

L

了	le	a particle

M

妈妈	māma	mum, mummy
吗	ma	an interrogative particle
面包	miànbāo	bread

N

那	nà	that
你	nǐ	you (single)

P

皮球	píqiú	ball
苹果	píngguǒ	apple

S

什么	shénme	what
是	shì	to be
手	shǒu	hand

S

书	shū	book
书包	shūbāo	satchel
叔叔	shūshu	uncle
树	shù	tree

T

他	tā	he, him
她	tā	she, her
太阳	tàiyáng	the sun

W

| 我 | wǒ | I, we |
| 我们 | wǒmen | we, us |

X

下	xià	to fall (of rain, snow, etc.)
学	xué	to learn
雪	xuě	snow

Y

眼睛	yǎnjing	eye
要	yào	to want
衣服	yīfu	clothes
有	yǒu	to have

Z

再见	zàijiàn	bye-bye, good-bye
这	zhè	this
中国	Zhōngguó	China

辅导材料

第1课

1．汉语的音节大多由声母（音节开头的辅音）和韵母（其余的部分）构成。如 ba 中的 b 是声母，a 是韵母；ge 中的 g 是声母，e 是韵母。

2．b、d、g 是不送气音，发音时口腔呼出的气流比较弱。

3．汉语是有声调的语言，每个音节不但音素要读准，而且声调也要读正确，否则就会产生意义上的误解。如 mā（妈），mǎ（马）等。

普通话有四个基本声调，声调符号是：第一声（ˉ）、第二声（ˊ）、第三声（ˇ）和第四声（ˋ）。调号画在元音上（元音 i 上有调号时，小点要去掉）。如 gē，dì 等。

四个声调可以用下图来表示：

| 第一声 | 第二声 | 第三声 | 第四声 |
| 高平 | 升 | 先降后升 | 降 |

本课先介绍第一声和第四声。

普通话里还有一种轻声，读得又轻又短。轻声不标调号，如 bàba，māma。

4．汉字是汉语的书写符号。一个音节写成一个汉字。汉字是由、一 丿 乀等基本笔画组成的。

第2课

1．汉语有的音节只有韵母，没有声母，如 ā。

2．汉语的韵母，有的是单元音，如 a、i、e、o；有的是复合元音，如 ao；有的是元音加鼻辅音，如 in。

一个音节的韵母有两个或两个以上的元音时，调号标在其中的主要元音（即响度大的元音上），如"hǎo"。

3．"āyí"一般为小孩或年轻人对跟自己母亲同辈的妇女的称呼。"bóbo"和"shūshu"（见第八课）都是用来称呼父辈男子的。"bóbo"常常用于称呼比自己父亲年岁大的男子，有更尊敬的意思。

4．"...hǎo"是汉语中使用较多的问候语，早上、中午、下午、晚上见面时都可以用。

"nín"是第二人称"nǐ"（见第七课）的尊称，小孩对成人说话一般应称"nín"。

第 4 课

p、t 是跟 b、d 相对的送气音，发音时必须用力吐出气流。

第 5 课

1．k 是跟 g 相对的的送气音，发音时必须用力吐出气流。

2．动词谓语句的否定形式，一般是在动词前面加上副词"bù"，如："Wǒ bù hē kāfēi."（I don't want coffee.）

"bù"单用或在第一、二、三声前读第四声，在第四声（或由第四声变来的轻声）前读第二声，如"bú yào"，"bù hǎo"。

第 6 课

1．zh、ch 是一组相对的不送气音和送气音。

2．韵母 i 在 zh、ch、sh、r 后读 [ʅ]，不能读成 [i]。韵母 i [i] 永远不会出现在这些声母的后边。

3．韵母 iu 跟声母相拼时，调号标在 u 上，如"niú"。

4．陈述句句尾加上语气助词 ma 就成了一般疑问句，如"Gēge yào niúnǎi"变成一般疑问句就是："Gēge yào niúnǎi ma?"

第 8 课

比较熟悉的同辈人之间或是长辈对晚辈问好，用"Nǐ hǎo"。

第 9 课

1．z、c 是一组相对的不送气音和送气音。韵母 i 在 z、c、s 后读 [ɿ]，不能读成 [i]。韵母 i [i] 永远不会出现在这些声母的后边。

2．在用疑问代词提问的疑问句中，疑问代词的位置，跟它所代表的陈述句中相对应的部分的位置一样，如："Zhè shì shénme?" "Zhè shì chá."

第 10 课

"是"字句的否定形式是"bú shì"，如："Nà bú shì huā."

第 11 课

两个三声字连在一起时，前一个三声字要读成第二声，如"wǒ yǒu..."实际读成"wó yǒu..."，"yǒu yǐzi"实际读成"yóu yǐzi"。

第 12 课

j、q 是一组相对的不送气音和送气音。

第 13 课

"有"字句的否定形式是在"yǒu"字前加副词"méi"，如"Wǒ méiyǒu píqiú"。

第 14 课

1．a、o、e 开头的音节连接在其他音节后面时，为了使音节界限清楚，要用隔音符号（'）隔开，如"Tiān'ānmén"。

2．定语一定要放在它所修饰的词语的前边，如"Zhōngguó guóqí"。

3．本课"Answer the questions"里的两个问题，要求用肯定句回答。

第 15 课

ü 及由 ü 开头的韵母和 j、q、x、y 相拼时，ü 上的两点省去，如"xuě"，"yǔ"。

第 17 课

韵母 ui 跟声母相拼时，调号标在 i 上，如"zuǐ"。

第 18 课

1．韵母 er 有时跟其他韵母结合成儿化韵母，儿化韵母的拼写法是在原韵母之后加"r"，如"shǒutàor"、"shǒujuànr"。

2．代词或名词作定语表示领属关系，后边一般都要用结构助词"de"，如"wǒ de yīfu"、"dìdi de kùzi"。

第 19 课

在会话中，当语言环境清楚时，为了避免重复，句子的主语、宾语有时省略，如本课中出现的：

Nǐ yào ma?　（Nǐ yào bǐ ma?）

Yào.　　　　（Wǒ yào bǐ.）

Gěi nǐ.　　　（Wǒ gěi nǐ bǐ.）

Teacher's Notes

Lesson One

1. A syllable in Chinese is usually composed of an initial, which is a consonant that begins the syllable and a final, which makes up the rest of the syllable. In the syllable "ba" or "ge", for instance, "b" and "g" are the initials while "a" and "e" are the finals.

2. "B, d, g" are consonants somewhat similar to English, but slightly weaker.

3. Chinese is a tonal language in which every syllable has one of four distinctive tones generally. To avoid misunderstanding, the tone as well as the initial and final of each syllable should be pronounced correctly. For example, "mā" means "mother", while "mǎ" means "horse".

The four basic tones in modern standard Chinese (or putonghua, the common speech) are represented respectively by the following tone marks: " ˉ " (the first tone), " ′ " (the second tone), " ˇ " (the third tone), and " ` " (the fourth tone). The tone mark is placed above the vowel sound, e.g., "gē"; note that the dot over the vowel "i" should be omitted if the tone mark of a syllable is placed above it, e.g., "dì".

The four tones may be illustrated as follows:

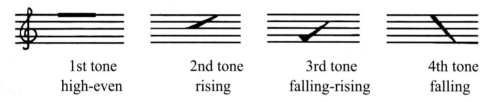

| 1st tone | 2nd tone | 3rd tone | 4th tone |
| high-even | rising | falling-rising | falling |

The 1st and 4th tones are dealt with in this lesson.

There are some syllables in modern standard Chinese (putonghua) the tones of which are pronounced both weak and short, and known as the neutral tone and is shown by the absence of a tone mark, e.g., the second syllables of "bàba", "māma".

4. Chinese characters, the written symbols of the Chinese language, are constituted of several basic strokes, such as " ˋ , 一 , | , ノ , ＼ ". In Chinese, one syllable stands for one character.

Lesson Two

1. Some syllables in Chinese may be formed with only a final and no initial, e.g., "ā".

2. The final may be a simple vowel, e.g., "a, i, e, o", a compound vowel, e.g., "ao" or a vowel followed by a nasal consonant, e.g., "in".

When the final of a syllable is composed of two or more vowels, the tone mark should be placed above the main vowel (namely the one pronounced with the mouth widest open), e.g., "hǎo".

3. "Āyí" is usually used by children or young people to address women of their mother's generation, while "bóbo" and "shūshu" (see Lesson 8) are used to address men of one's father's generation. "Bóbo" is a term often used to show respect to a man elder than one's father.

4. "...hǎo" is an expression of common greeting used in the morning, at noon, in the

afternoon or evening.

"Nín" is the polite equivalent of "nǐ", the personal pronoun in the second person singular (see Lesson 7). When children address adults, "nín" should be used instead of "nǐ".

Lesson Four

Corresponding to the unaspirated "b,d","p,t" are aspirated consonants, which explode with a strong puff of air.

Lesson Five

1. The initial "k" is an aspirated consonant corresponding to the unaspirated "g". When it is pronounced, breath should be puffed out strongly.

2. To make a sentence with a verbal predicate negative, the adverb "bù" is usually put before the predicative verb, e.g., "Wǒ bú yào kāfēi." (I don't want coffee.)

The word "bù" is pronounced in the 4th tone when it stands alone or precedes a 1st, 2nd or 3rd tone, but is pronounced in the 2nd tone when it precedes a 4th tone (or a neutral tone that was originally a 4th tone), e.g., "bú yào", "bù hǎo".

Lesson Six

1. The initial "ch" is an aspirated consonant corresponding to the unaspirated "zh".

2. After the initial "zh, ch, sh" or "r", the final "i" stands for the vowel [ɿ] and care must be taken that not to pronounce it as the final "i [i]", which is never found after "zh, ch, sh" or "r".

3. When the final "iu" is preceded by an initial, the tone mark is placed on "u", e.g., "niú".

4. The same word order is used in questions as in statements. A statement can be turned into a general question by just adding the modal particle "ma" at the end of it. For instance, we can change "Gēge yào niúnǎi. "(My elder brother wants milk.) into "Gēge yào niúnǎi ma? " (Does your elder brother want milk?)

Lesson Eight

"Nǐ hǎo" is a common greeting used among people of the same generation or by the older to the younger.

Lesson Nine

1. The initial "c" is an aspirated consonant corresponding to the unaspirated "z". After the initials "z", "c" and "s", the final "i", stands for the vowel [ʅ] and cannot be pronounced as the vowel [i], which is never found after "z", "c" or "s".

2. A question containing an interrogative pronoun in Chinese has the same word order as that of a statement. The interrogative pronoun in a question is put in the same place as the part questioned in a statement, e.g., "Zhè shì shénme?" (What's this?) "Zhè shì chá." (It's tea.)

Lesson Ten

A sentence with "shì" as its predicative verb is made negative by changing "shì" into "bú shì", e.g., "Nà bú shì huā. " (That is not a flower.)

Lesson Eleven

A third tone before another third tone should be changed into a second tone, e.g., "wǒ yǒu..." is actually pronounced as "wó yǒu...", and "yǒu yǐzi" is "yóu yǐzi."

Lesson Twelve

The initial "q" is an aspirated consonant corresponding to the unaspirated "j".

Lesson Thirteen

A sentence with "yǒu" as its predicative verb is made negative by adding the adverb "méi" before "yǒu", e.g., "wǒ méiyǒu píqiú." (I don't have a ball.)

Lesson Fourteen

1. When a syllable beginning with "a" "o" or "e" follows another syllable, a dividing mark " ' " should be put in between to make the division of the two syllables more clear, e.g., "Tiān'ānmén".

2. In Chinese, an attributive must precede what it qualifies, e.g., "Zhōngguó guóqí" (Chinese national flag).

3. Key to 'Answer the questions': "Zhè shì kuàizi." "Zhè shì zhuōzi."

Lesson Fifteen

When appearing after "j, q, x, y", the umlaut of " ü " or compound final beginning with " ü " is omitted, e.g., "xuě", "yǔ".

Lesson Seventeen

When the final "ui" is preceded by an initial, the tone mark is placed on "i", e.g., "zuǐ".

Lesson Eighteen

1. The final "er" is sometimes attached to another final to form a retroflex final, which is formed by adding the letter "r" to the original final, e.g., "shǒutàor" (gloves), "shǒujuànr" (handkerchief).

2. When a pronoun or a noun is used attributively to show possession, it must take after it the structural particle "de", as in "wǒ de yīfu" (my dress), "dìdi de kùzi" (my younger brother's trousers).

Lesson Nineteen

In a conversation the subject or the object of a sentence is often omitted to avoid repetition when it is clear from the context.

E.g., Nǐ yào ma? (Nǐ yào bǐ ma?)
  Yào. (Wǒ yào bǐ.)
  Gěi ni. (Wǒ gěi ni bǐ.)

图 书 推 荐
Highlights

快乐儿童汉语 (全两册)

Fun Chinese for Children (2 volumes)

汉英 Chinese–English edition

208×275mm，92pp/each

ISBN 9787800529276

ISBN 9787800529283

¥46.00/each

Rights sold: Russian

- 适合以英语为母语的学龄前儿童学习汉语的初级读本，共两册，第一册17课，第二册21课。
- 从汉语拼音开始学汉语，形式活泼，语言生动，图文并茂，好学好说，即学即用，学一句可以用一句。
- Elementary readers and textbooks for non-native speaking children to learn Chinese as a foreign language.
- This series consists of 2 volumes. The first includes 17 lessons, and the second 21 lessons.
- Starting from pinyin. Detailed descriptions of tones are given.
- Using dialogues applicable to children's everyday life.
- Games and funny cartoons are provided.

- -

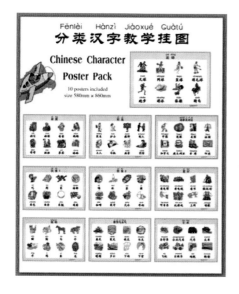

分类汉字教学挂图

Chinese Character Poster Pack
(10 posters)

580×860mm/each

ISBN 9787802002982

¥118.00

All rights available.

- 《分类汉字教学挂图》共10张，包含国家及地区、职业、交通、爱好、家庭、动物、季节与天气、饮食、运动等最基本的汉字和注音。
- Includes ten posters on countries and regions, occupations, vehicles, hobbies, family members, animals, seasons and weather, food and sport.
- All the words are illustrated. The posters can be used to decorate classrooms.

责任编辑：韩　颖
英　译：张　耘
封面设计：王新乐
印刷监制：佟汉冬

图书在版编目（CIP）数据

新儿童汉语·1 / 刘珣，张亚军，丁永寿编著 . —— 北京 ：华语教学出版社，2011
ISBN 978-7-5138-0082-2

Ⅰ. ①新… Ⅱ.①刘… ②张… ③丁… Ⅲ.①汉语－对外汉语教学－儿童教育－教材
Ⅳ.① H195.4

中国版本图书馆 CIP 数据核字 (2011) 第 098548 号

新儿童汉语·1

刘珣　张亚军　丁永寿 编著

*

© 华语教学出版社
华语教学出版社出版
（中国北京百万庄大街 24 号　　邮政编码　100037）
电话 :(86)10-68320585, 68997826
传真 :(86)10-68997826, 68320585
网址 ：www.sinolingua.com.cn
电子信箱 ：hyjx@sinolingua.com.cn
三河市汇鑫印务有限公司印刷
2011 年（16 开）第 1 版
（汉英）
ISBN 978-7-5138-0082-2
定价 ：39.00 元